BOMBERS

Modern Military Techniques

MODERN MILITARY TECHNIQUES
BOMBERS

Malcolm V. Lowe

Illustrations by
Peter Sarson & Tony Bryan

 Lerner Publications Company • Minneapolis

Library of Congress Cataloging-in-Publication Data

Lowe, Malcolm V.
   Bombers.

   (Modern military techniques)
   Includes index.
   Summary: Surveys modern bombers and attack aircraft,
discussing recent developments in design, weapons, and
tactics.
   1. Bombers—Juvenile literature. 2. Attack planes—
Juvenile literature. [1. Bombers. 2. Attack planes.
3. Airplanes, Military] I. Sarson, Peter, ill.
II. Bryan, Tony, ill. III. Title. IV. Series.
UG1242.B6L68   1987   623.74'63   86-10696
ISBN 0-8225-1381-1 (lib. bdg.)

Manufactured in the United States of America

1 2 3 4 5 6 7 8 9 10 95 94 93 92 91 90 89 88 87

CONTENTS

1 Bombers and Attack Aircraft

With a huge warload compared to that carried by World War II bombers and with great destructive power, the modern long-range bomber is able to strike at targets deep within the enemy's own country. Some bombers have specific long-range tasks, such as the anti-shipping missions performed by the Soviet Tupolev Tu-26 "Backfire," an aircraft that is from the recent generation of supersonic swing-wing bombers.

Bombers are much larger than attack aircraft, which generally operate over shorter ranges. Modern attack aircraft take many forms from the relatively light and slow-flying aircraft used over the battlefield to very sophisticated types operating miles behind the enemy lines, sometimes with the capability of nuclear strike. The Grumman A-6 Intruder is one of the best attack aircraft in the world, which, due to its comprehensive avionics, can carry out precision attacks either in daylight or at night in any weather conditions, even on targets that are exceptionally difficult to find.

A very different approach to attack aircraft design and employment is exemplified by the Dassault-Breguet/Dornier Alpha Jet. This aircraft can be used for light attack missions with a warload much smaller than that carried by larger attack aircraft. Compared to the A-6 Intruder, it has a comparatively limited avionics fit and so cannot perform longer-range precision attacks in any weather conditions. But like other small attack aircraft, it has a useful load-carrying capability for close battlefield support, for which its avionics are quite adequate.

Sometimes a bomber or attack aircraft type is modified to produce a sub-variant that can perform completely different roles, such as electronic warfare or photoreconnaissance. When retired from front-line service, older designs may also be converted and used in this way. An example is the BAC Canberra, a British bomber design of the post-World War II years, a photoreconnaissance version of which is still in service with the Royal Air Force.

The Boeing B-52 Stratofortress has been in US Air Force service for thirty years, and like other bombers currently in service, can carry nuclear weapons as well as conventional bombs.

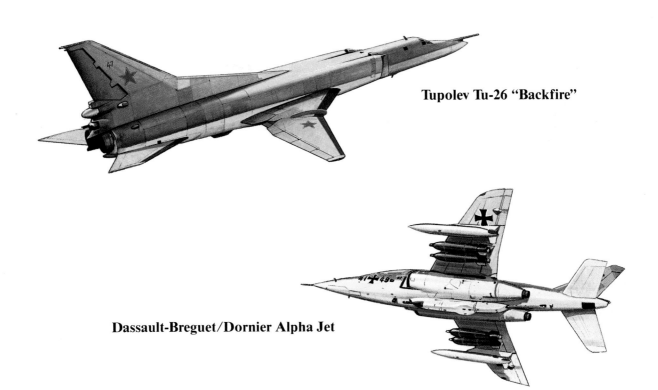

Tupolev Tu-26 "Backfire"

Dassault-Breguet/Dornier Alpha Jet

Grumman A-6 Intruder

BAC Canberra PR Mk 9

2 The Modern Bomber

The Rockwell B-1B is the West's newest bomber to see service. It will be fully operational with the US Air Force by the later 1980's and features the most up-to-date avionics and systems available. Current plans are that 100 of these sophisticated long-range bombers will be built, and in US Air Force service, they will replace the aging B-52 Stratofortress. The first B-1 made its maiden flight in 1974. The aircraft was first envisioned as a high-level nuclear bomber, but the design has since been refined and the aircraft's role switched to the comparatively safer but more demanding low-level penetration role. The B-1's carefully streamlined and blended shape, allied with such important avionics as terrain-following radar, makes it ideal for this. Like other modern bombers, the B-1B is able to carry both conventional and nuclear weapons inside its fuselage and externally.

Specifications

Wingspan (wings swept)	: 78.67 feet (23.84 m)
Wingspan (wings unswept)	: 137.51 feet (41.67 m)
Length	: 151.07 feet (45.78 m)
Height	: 33.79 feet (10.24 m)
Wing area (wings unswept)	: 217.44 sq. yards (181.2 m²)
Empty weight	: 159,665 lbs. (72,575 kg)
Maximum take-off weight	: 476,000 lbs. (216,364 kg)
Maximum speed—	
over 11,000 m	: Mach 1.2 +
at 152 m	: Mach 0.99
Service ceiling	: 49,500 feet + (15,000 m +)
Range (with maximum internal fuel)	: 6,759 miles (11,265 km +)
Warload	: 79,834 lbs. (36,288 kg)

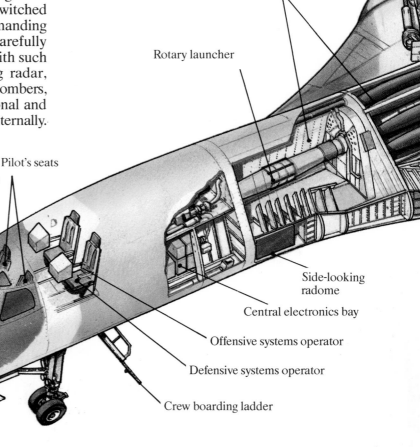

Weapons bay

Rotary launcher

Pilot's seats

Structural mode control vane

Forward electronics bay

In-flight refueling coupling

Forward radar

Radome

Side-looking radome

Central electronics bay

Offensive systems operator

Defensive systems operator

Crew boarding ladder

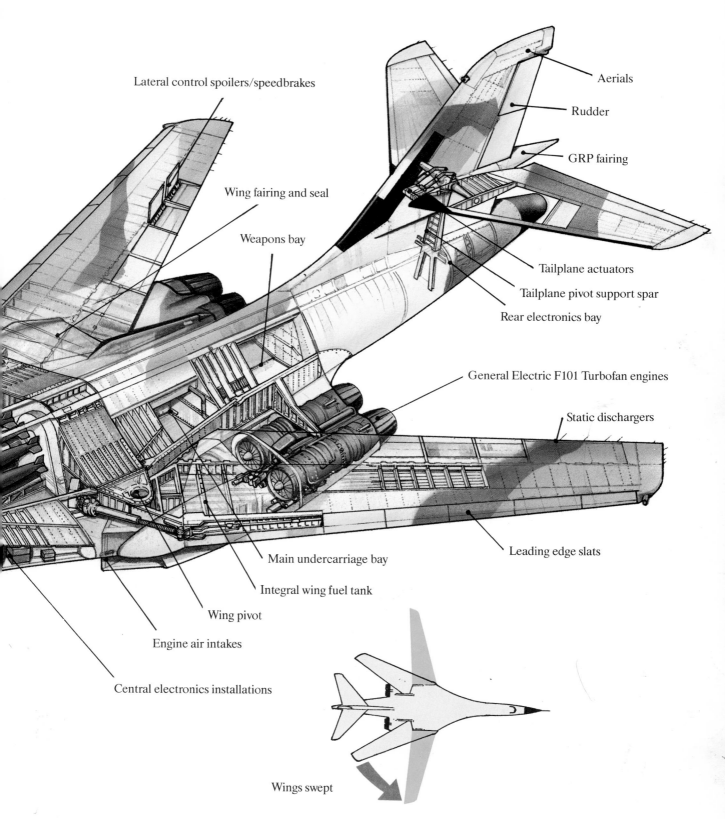

Lateral control spoilers/speedbrakes

Wing fairing and seal

Weapons bay

Aerials

Rudder

GRP fairing

Tailplane actuators

Tailplane pivot support spar

Rear electronics bay

General Electric F101 Turbofan engines

Static dischargers

Leading edge slats

Main undercarriage bay

Integral wing fuel tank

Wing pivot

Engine air intakes

Central electronics installations

Wings swept

Wings unswept

3
Bomber Design Features (1)

Modern bombers are very large, long-range aircraft able to strike at strategic targets such as industrial complexes and cities deep inside an enemy country. Today, they are only operated by superpowers and a few other countries who in times of war might wish to strike at such targets and can afford these very expensive aircraft.

The Soviet Tupolev Tu-95 "Bear" is typical of these giant-sized aircraft with a wingspan of over 168.3 feet (51m). It is unusual in being powered by turboprop engines rather than jets, which give it a very long unrefueled range by being fuel-efficient. It also features an aerodynamically clean and efficient swept wing. Several of the Soviet bombers have versions that perform an extra role in carrying out anti-ship missions with large air-to-surface missiles. For this, the aircraft carry a massive nose radome featuring a long-range radar for detection of potential targets.

Weapon carrying

The carriage of weapons by modern bombers is closely related to the size of these weapons, which in the case of missiles may be considerable. Many bombers have provision for carrying some weapons internally, as does the B-1B, but a popular arrangement in several designs is to carry one large missile recessed below the fuselage, while further missiles are carried on large pylons beneath the wings. The Soviet Tupolev Tu-26 "Backfire" bomber uses this arrangement.

For those aircraft featuring a bomb bay, and where the missile size is not too large, it is possible to carry several missiles within a relatively

The weapon carrying arrangement of the Soviet Tupolev Tu-26 "Backfire" bomber

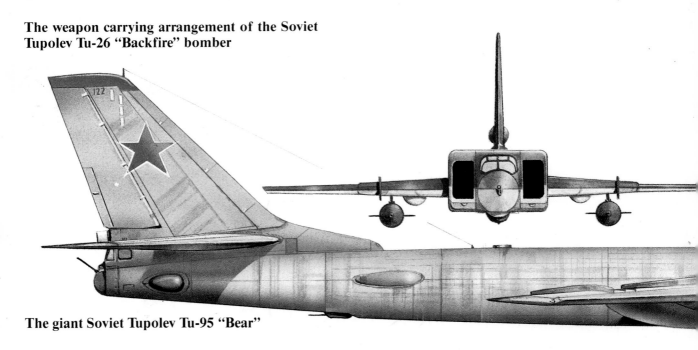

The giant Soviet Tupolev Tu-95 "Bear"

small space by mounting them on a rotary launcher. This is carried in the bomb bay of the B-52 and the B-1B and can carry the Boeing AGM-69A SRAM and AGM-86B. Up to eight missiles can be mounted on the launcher in a similar fashion to the way bullets are loaded in a revolver. Each missile is launched in turn, the launcher rotating each time to select the next missile for launch.

Defensive armament

Like bombers of the past, some modern bombers still retain a defensive armament of guns in specially-designed gun turrets. The remote-controlled tail-gun position of a B-52 Stratofortress uses radomes for the search and tracking radars that detect and follow potential targets, giving the gunner, who sits well forward of the turret, correct guidance for the guns to fire. The effectiveness of this defensive armament was displayed during the Vietnam War when B-52 gunners shot down a number of MiG fighters attacking their aircraft.

Above right: The remote-controlled tail-gun position of a B-52 Stratofortress

Right: A rotary launcher carrying SRAMs in a B-52 bomber

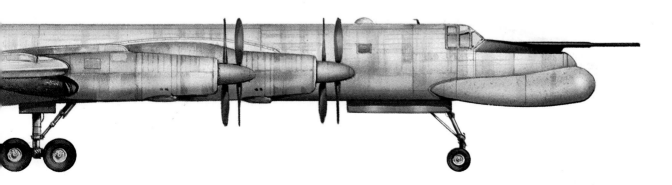

4
Bomber Design Features (2)

Electronic countermeasures equipment

As well as defensive guns, an impressive array of electronic countermeasures (ECM) equipment is carried by both US and Soviet bombers. It is used to counter new advances in the detection of aircraft and the guidance of ground-to-air and air-to-air missiles. Other extras that have been added to the basic B-52 design include the LLTV and FLIR equipment for operations in poor visibility or at night.

Special features of cruise missile carriers

The air-launched cruise missile is a relatively new weapon available for use by bombers. This development in weapon technology has had an important effect on arms limitations talks between the superpowers, making it necessary to identify the aircraft carrying these weapons. Not all B-52s are converted to carry cruise missiles, so in order that Soviet surveillance satellites can distinguish between ordinary B-52s and those that carry cruise missiles, the later carry special wing fairings that can be identified by these satellites.

Crew escape features

A novel feature incorporated in the design of one particular bomber, the swing-wing General Dynamics FB-111A, is the substitution of standard ejector seats for the crew, as found in most modern combat aircraft, by an entire cockpit capsule. In the event of an emergency, the entire capsule can be fired out of the aircraft by the crew. The capsule descends back to earth, suspended below parachutes. A useful feature of the capsule is that it can land on water as well as on land. The FB-111A is the bomber version of an attack aircraft design, the standard F-111, which also carries this novel escape system.

ECM antennae and related avionics carried by the B-52G, a great deal of which has been added on during its long service life

Swing-wing designs

The swing-wing or variable-geometry design has become increasingly important in recent bomber construction; several US and Soviet bombers use this design innovation. Variable geometry allows the aircraft's wing sweep to be altered to suit the particular flight profile being undertaken. A fully extended wing, especially if fitted with full-span slats and flaps, gives excellent short-airfield performance, allowing even a big aircraft like the B-1B to fly out of comparatively small airfields carrying a large load, a maneuver requiring slow landing and take off speeds. The aircraft can cruise at subsonic speeds with the wings spread, thus saving fuel. While with swings swept back, it can fly at high speed, a very useful feature for a fast dash to the target at low level.

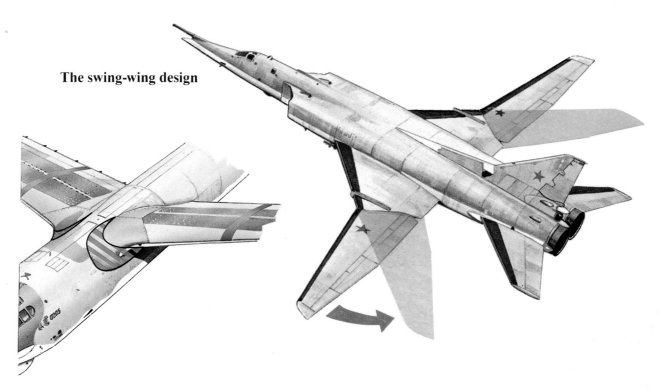

The swing-wing design

Special wing fairings for cruise-missile carrying B-52

The crew escape capsule carried by the F-111

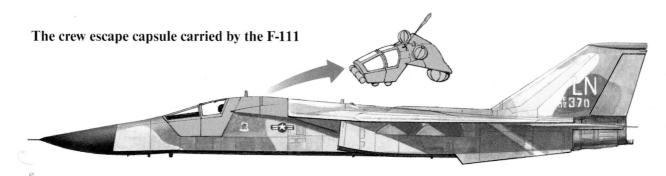

5 Bomber Weapons

Up to the end of the Second World War and beyond, the main type of weapon carried by bombers was the free-fall bomb. Since then, the missile has been fully developed and gained great importance, especially as it is able to strike at a target accurately from a great distance. Nevertheless, the free-fall bomb of both the nuclear and the conventional type has remained an important part of the bomber's weaponry.

Free-fall bombs

On some occasions, as in the war in Vietnam during the 1960's and early 1970's, bombers are called upon to drop conventional free-fall bombs. These can be dropped from great heights, or if dropped at low level can carry retarding devices in their tail units to slow them after release, allowing the aircraft to be some distance away from the blast when the bombs explode. Very different both in size and in explosive potential are free-fall nuclear bombs. Like conventional bombs, they can be dropped from considerable heights if need be. In the West, several types of nuclear bomb have been developed.

Missiles

Among the weapons carried by bombers, missiles are very important in allowing the bomber to stand off from the target; that is, to launch its missiles many miles from the target, so avoiding the need to fly close to the target's defenses and risk being shot down. Missiles carried by bombers are mainly large weapons, often powered by a rocket motor. They usually carry a nuclear warhead, in some cases a large warhead of up to 350 kt or more, though conventional high-explosive warheads can be carried instead by some missiles, these generally being of some 2,200 pounds (1,000 kg). Both the Soviet Union and the US have a large number of missiles available for use with their bombers.

An important weapon used by the US is the Boeing AGM-69A SRAM, an accurate missile with a range of over 96 miles (160 km) at high level. It is guided by means of inertial navigation and can

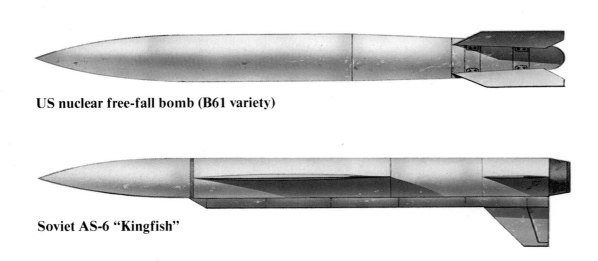

US nuclear free-fall bomb (B61 variety)

Soviet AS-6 "Kingfish"

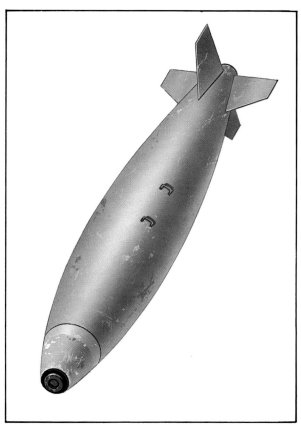

be used to attack strategic targets including cities or industrial complexes, as well as striking at defensive installations.

The Soviet Union deploys several missile types, which could be used as nuclear strike weapons against strategic targets, anti-shipping, and anti-radar defense suppression: the AS-4 "Kitchen" and AS-6 "Kingfish," the latter carried by the Soviet Tupolev Tu-16 "Badger-C" bomber. Both are multi-role missiles, guided by inertial navigation for flight direction and in most versions radar for terminal guidance; both can carry a conventional warhead or a nuclear warhead of 350 kt.

Left: US conventional free-fall bomb

Below: A Soviet Tupolev Tu-16 "Badger-C" bomber carrying AS-6 missiles

6
The Air-Launched Cruise Missile

One of the most important advances in bomber weapons has been the development of the Air-Launched Cruise Missile (ALCM). This weapon is a special adaptation of the basic air-launched missile concept. As with other missiles, it has guidance systems that allow it to find its target very accurately over many miles, but a particular advantage is that it can do this while flying very close to the ground following the terrain of the land. By doing so, it has a greater chance of reaching the target because it can fly below the enemy's radar cover, so avoiding detection, and it requires no link by radar or guidance means from the bomber after it is launched, so avoiding the possibility of having such communications jammed by the enemy and betraying the weapon's position.

Instead, it has a self-contained guidance system, which features inertial navigation linked with terrain-contour matching (tercom). Inertial navigation is also a feature of the missiles already described, but the ALCM generally uses this facility by itself only on the flight's early stages, which are usually over the sea. Once over land, the missile's navigation system is then continually updated by the tercom equipment, an important part of which is a radar altimeter.

This provides continuous height data about the missile's flight, giving a profile picture of the ground being flown over which the missile's avionics then compare with stored maps and other information in the missile's memory bank. These maps contain preplanned details of the missile's

proposed flight path to the target, and using the tercom equipment, the missile's avionics can automatically check that the missile is on the correct course for the target, the location of which has already been fed into the missile's systems. Any necessary adjustments to its flight path are then made through the onboard auto-pilot systems. It can also be preprogrammed with evasive maneuvers to confuse the enemy as to its intended target. The ALCM is potentially a very accurate weapon, difficult to detect and shoot down, and with its great range, it can strike at strategic targets deep within the enemy's country, even if launched hundreds of miles outside enemy territory.

The ALCM first entered service with the US Air Force on its B-52Gs in December 1982 in the

Boeing AGM-86B Air-Launched Cruise Missile (ALCM)

Specifications

Length	: 20.576 feet (6.235 m)
Wingspan (wings extended)	: 12.071 feet (3.658 m)
Diameter	: 2.287 feet (0.693 m)
Launch weight	: 2,819 lbs. (1,281.4 kg)
Maximum speed	: 483 mph (805 km/h)
Maximum range	: 1,500 miles (2,500 km +)
Warhead	: W80 200 kt yield nuclear

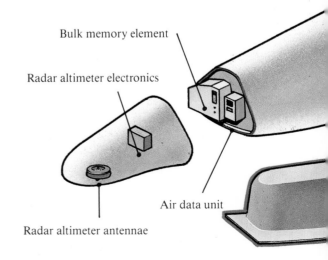

Bulk memory element

Radar altimeter electronics

Air data unit

Radar altimeter antennae

form of the AGM-86B. It is one of several types of cruise missile, the other main types being launched from submarine and ground launchers. It is possible to strike at an enemy from a variety of locations and situations using these weapons, causing the enemy major problems in trying to stop them. The US Air Force requires over 4,000 ALCMs, both the B-52 and B-1 being able to carry the missile on internal and external launchers; when carried by these aircraft before launch, the missile's wings, tail surfaces, and engine inlet are folded.

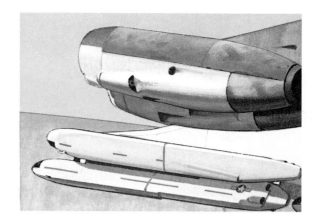

Right: Air-launched cruise missiles mounted on the standard B-52 wing pylon in their folded state

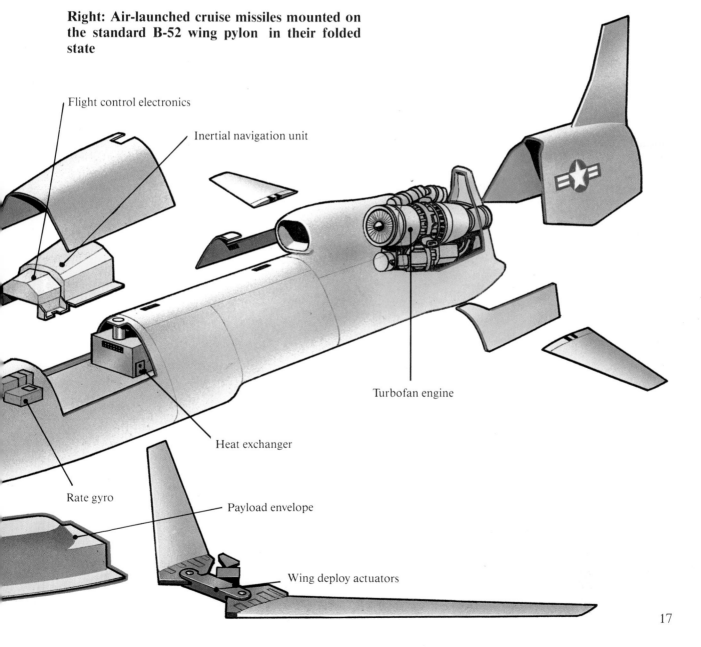

Flight control electronics

Inertial navigation unit

Turbofan engine

Heat exchanger

Rate gyro

Payload envelope

Wing deploy actuators

7
Bomber Missions

The B-52 radar-guided to its target flying at high level

Missions with conventional and cruise missiles

During the Second World War and for some time afterwards, the main type of bombing mission involved flying at medium to high altitude to the target, dropping bombs on it from a considerable height using visual or radar sighting (the latter in its infancy during the Second World War), and then flying back at high altitude to bases. With

A B-52 launching a cruise missile from outside the country, while a B-1B penetrates at low level, flying towards the target and launching a SRAM

the advent of effective surface-to-air missiles and defensive radars with considerable accuracy, this type of mission became far too dangerous. Formations of bombers at high level were a sitting target for the enemy's defenses.

Today, the high-level mission would only be used against targets that were lightly defended or had defenses that could be overwhelmed, or made relatively ineffective, by jamming using ECM. During the Vietnam War, B-52s were used in this way to bomb targets deep inside North Vietnam from heights of over 6 miles (10 km). Radar guidance was used to guide the bombers to their targets, bomb release being made after such factors as position of target, wind drift of bombs after launch, and flight characteristics of the weapons carried had been taken into consideration.

Against heavily defended targets, the modern bomber can employ one of two main types of flight profile. It can penetrate the enemy's defenses by flying as low as possible using TFR to come in under the enemy's radar cover, either dropping conventional retarded bombs over the target or launching a short-range stand-off missile such as the SRAM at the target and at defenses located on the way to the target. The B-1B would be particularly well suited to such a mission, due in part to its specially blended design, which would be difficult for the enemy to detect by radar or visual means.

In the second main type of mission, aircraft armed with the ALCM have a great advantage in that the missile itself has a considerable range. It is thus possible to launch it without the bomber having to fly over enemy territory, the missile itself being able to guide itself to the target after launch as long as correct instructions for flying to the target and locating it have been fed into the missile's avionics systems prior to launch. The bomber can be further protected by being shielded by ECM aircraft, as indeed was the case during the Vietnam War, and can fly long distances to its launch area by being in-flight refueled on the way.

8
Anti-Shipping Bomber Missions

Soviet anti-shipping missions

The large anti-ship missiles described on page 14 can be used by Soviet navy aviation bombers as a weapon against major naval targets such as surface fleets. One of these substantial missiles, to which a nuclear warhead could be fitted, has the capability of demolishing a large shipping target such as an aircraft carrier. As such, these missiles are different from the anti-ship weapons for use by maritime attack aircraft, which are smaller missiles effective against warships, but requiring several direct hits to sink such a large target as an aircraft carrier unless a lucky hit in a particularly vulnerable spot is achieved.

The AS-6 "Kingfish" anti-ship missile can approach its target at low level using inertial guidance and active radar homing when nearing the target, but a more likely flight path would be a high-level approach. In this configuration, the missile again uses inertial guidance, climbing to around 10.8 miles (18 km) after launch, then dives on its target using active radar homing and increasing its speed to over Mach 3. In this flight profile, the missile has a range of over 300 miles (500 km).

The diagram on the right shows how a surface fleet might be attacked using these weapons in a coordinated strike. The surface ships are initially detected, then tracked by satellite surveillance, although various other means, such as surveillance ships disguised as trawlers, maritime patrol aircraft, and submarines, can be used with considerable effectiveness. The fleet is then attacked simultaneously from several different directions by missile-carrying bombers and submarines. The fleet has to counter all these varied attacks at once and so has its defenses split.

The anti-ship missiles give their launch aircraft stand off capability, keeping them well away from the fleet's defensive aircraft and weapons. Once launched and successfully guided to the target, it is very difficult for the defending fleet to destroy incoming missiles, especially if they have been sent in at high level and have started their dive onto the target, although jamming of the missile's radar is possible, and it can also be fired upon if spotted in time. Nevertheless, the high speed of this type of missile, and the general plan of attacking a surface fleet with submarines as well as aircraft and possibly using a large number of missiles, ensures that some may well get through to their targets.

"Backfire"

US anti-sub helicopter

Soviet intelligence collector ship

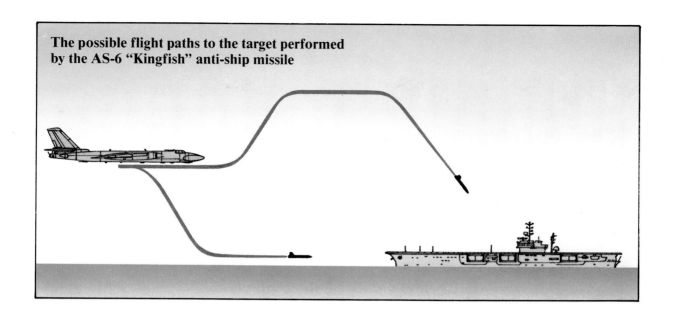

The possible flight paths to the target performed by the AS-6 "Kingfish" anti-ship missile

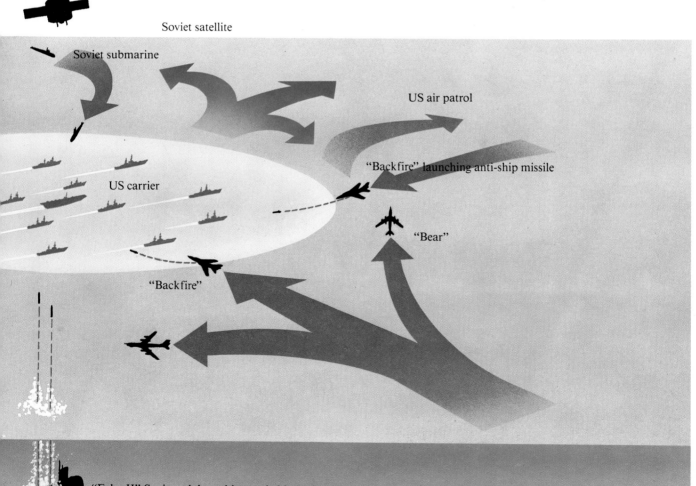

Soviet satellite

Soviet submarine

US air patrol

"Backfire" launching anti-ship missile

US carrier

"Bear"

"Backfire"

"Echo II" Soviet sub launching anti-ship cruise missile

9
The Modern Attack Aircraft

The Fairchild A-10A Thunderbolt II is in every respect an attack aircraft, designed and built for just that purpose. The type first flew in 1972, the product of a US requirement mainly as a result of combat experience in Vietnam, for a highly-maneuverable, heavily-armed and armored attack aircraft able to carry out devastating close support missions against such targets as enemy tanks and motorized vehicles. The aircraft's overall design is the result of the particular requirements of this type of mission. Special features include engines mounted high on the rear fuselage so as not to attract heat-seeking missiles fired from the

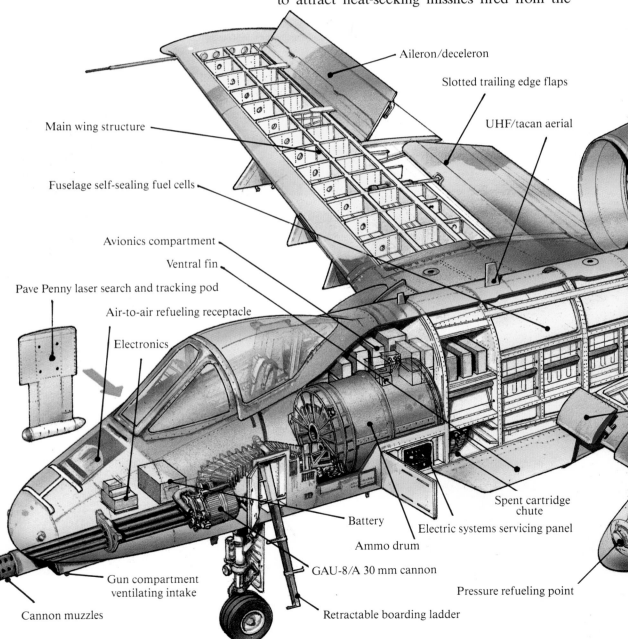

Aileron/deceleron

Slotted trailing edge flaps

UHF/tacan aerial

Main wing structure

Fuselage self-sealing fuel cells

Avionics compartment

Ventral fin

Pave Penny laser search and tracking pod

Air-to-air refueling receptacle

Electronics

Spent cartridge chute

Battery

Electric systems servicing panel

Ammo drum

Gun compartment ventilating intake

GAU-8/A 30 mm cannon

Pressure refueling point

Cannon muzzles

Retractable boarding ladder

ground through being "shielded" by the wings and tailplane, a generally well-protected airframe and cockpit, impressive firepower from its GAU-8/A rapid-fire cannon, and large external weapon-carrying ability. Over 700 A-10As have been procured by the US Air Force; the aircraft below belonging to the 81st Tactical Fighter Wing which is based in England.

Specifications

Wingspan	: 57.85 feet (17.53 m)
Length	: 53.66 feet (16.26 m)
Height	: 14.75 feet (4.47 m)
Wing area	: 56.41 sq. yards (47.01m²)
Empty weight	: 21,474 lbs. (9,761 kg)
Maximum takeoff weight	: 49,896 lbs. (22,680 kg)
Maximum speed at sea level	: 424 mph (706 km/h)
Service ceiling	: 34,898 m + (10,575 m +)
Range (with maximum internal fuel)	: 2,400 miles (4,000 km +)
Combat radius (on Close Air Support mission with 1.88 hour loiter plus reserves)	: 278 miles (463 km)
Warload (maximum load on 11 hardpoints)	: 15,969 miles (7,258 kg)

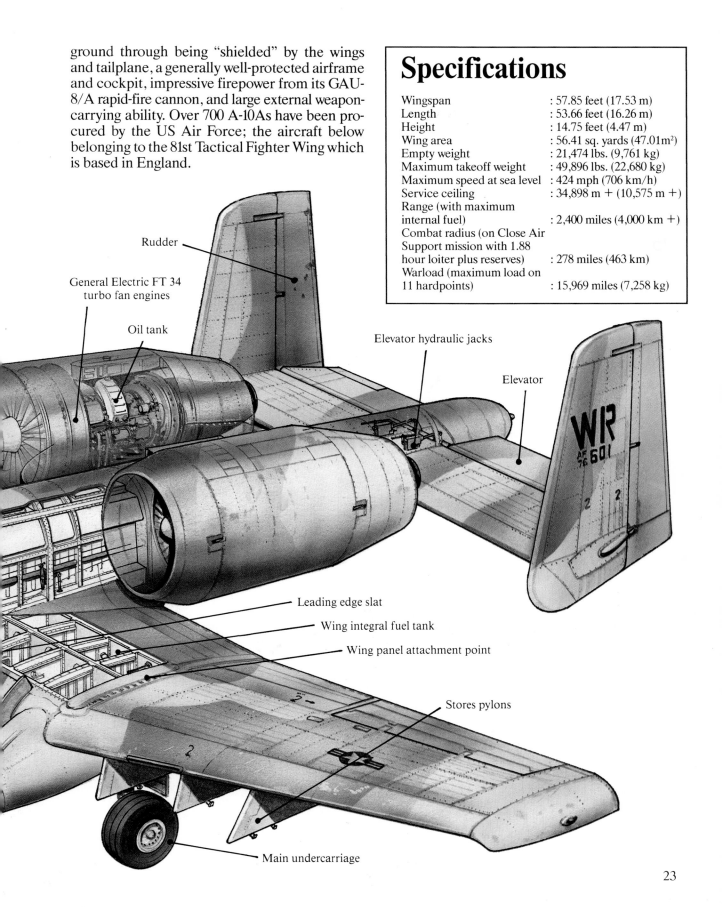

Rudder

General Electric FT 34 turbo fan engines

Oil tank

Elevator hydraulic jacks

Elevator

Leading edge slat

Wing integral fuel tank

Wing panel attachment point

Stores pylons

Main undercarriage

10 Attack Aircraft Design Features (1)

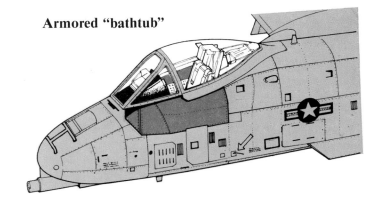

Armored "bathtub"

Armor protection

A very important factor in the design of attack aircraft is the protection of vital components from the ground fire that all attack aircraft are subjected to. Armor protection is built into these aircraft to protect such areas as fuel tanks, control linkages, and in and around the cockpit area. One of the most thoroughly protected aircraft to be built is the A-10A Thunderbolt II, and an example of this aircraft's protection is in the cockpit area, in which the pilot plus all his flight controls and related equipment are situated within an armored "bathtub." Some aircraft like the A-10A are so designed that even if they receive a direct hit from ground fire, they can often stay in the air and return safely to base.

Weapon carrying

The weapon-carrying capacity of many modern attack aircraft is very impressive, a wide range of air-to-ground missiles and bombs being available for use by most attack types. Unlike bombers, most attack aircraft carry their bombs and missiles externally on under-wing and under-fuselage pylons. The number of pylons can sometimes be substantial — up to eleven on the A-10A, for example, this aircraft's maximum external load of 15,967.6 pounds (7,258 kg) being similar to the bombload of the World War II Avro Lancaster heavy bomber.

Radar systems

A vitally important part of the avionics fit of attack aircraft tasked with longer-range low-level missions inside enemy territory, especially if the missions are carried out in bad weather or at night, is a terrain-following radar (TFR). Bombers such as the B-1B also carry this equipment for long-range penetration missions against strategic targets. The radar emits its beam ahead of the aircraft at the terrain over which it will fly, and corrective instructions to the aircraft's autopilot fly the aircraft over or around the terrain detected, but as close to it as safety permits. A radar altimeter is also vital, giving the aircraft's true altitude above the terrain over which it flies.

Gunship conversions

Among the most unusual attack aircraft to be found are the converted aircraft, usually

Terrain-following radar (TFR) of the F-111

transports, known as gunships. These arose out of operational requirements during the Vietnam War for an aircraft able to provide fire against ground targets to support friendly forces, often for long periods of time. The transport's long endurance and slow flying speeds allow it to keep on station above and around the scene of battle for many hours, and their armament of machine guns or

The under-wing and under-fuselage pylons that carry the weapons on an attack aircraft

even heavy cannons is vital for aiding hard-pressed ground forces. Targets can be designated by these ground forces or detected from the air by visual means or by using the aircraft's special radar, infra-red or LLTV.

The AC-130A gunship conversion of the famous Lockheed C-130 Hercules transport aircraft

11
Attack Aircraft Design Features (2)

Maritime attack features

The design of maritime patrol and attack aircraft may differ substantially from that of attack aircraft used only against land targets. The Lockheed S-3A Viking carrier-borne anti-submarine warfare (ASW) patrol and attack aircraft can search for and detect submerged submarines and attack them with a variety of suitable weapons. For detection and tracking purposes it carries radar, infra-red sensors, a selection of sonobuoys which can be dropped into the water to perform "passive" or "active" search for submarines, and a Magnetic Anomaly Detector (MAD) boom. Because the latter is sensitive to magnetic variations, the MAD equipment is positioned at the end of a boom to keep it as far as possible from the magnetic disturbance caused by the aircraft itself.

Target detection and Electronic countermeasures equipment

In such factors as target detection and the ability to hit even the most difficult targets with pin-point accuracy, today's attack aircraft have come a long way. Among the sophisticated equipment available for incorporation in modern attack aircraft, there is FLIR and LLTV for low-visibility attack and laser designators and seekers. The Pave Penny laser seeker, carried by the A-10A, is typical of the kind of seeker available for modern attack aircraft. This equipment's laser sensor searches for and locates laser energy reflected from a target that is being illuminated by a laser designator on the ground or from a Forward Air Control (FAC) aircraft, allowing the target to be precisely identified and attacked.

In addition to this targeting equipment, attack aircraft have to carry a large number of ECM systems in order to avoid being detected by enemy radars. These systems are used to jam the enemy radar, to give it false radar returns, and to prevent it from locking onto the attack aircraft. As they are much smaller than long-range bombers, attack aircraft carry some of this ECM equipment externally; typically in ECM pods, carried on the aircraft's normal under-wing or under-fuselage pylons.

Chaff and flares can also be carried to jam or decoy the enemy's radar and guided missiles aimed at the attack aircraft.

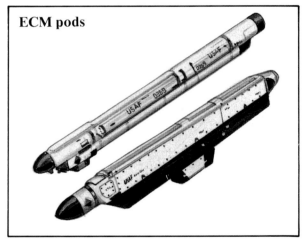

ECM pods

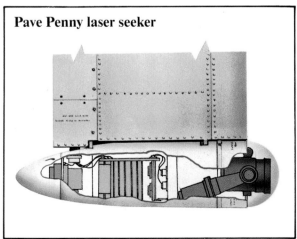

Pave Penny laser seeker

Two extra crew members (making four in total) are carried, plus a large amount of computer equipment to assimilate all the information from these various sensors.

On the larger maritime patrol aircraft, such as the French Dassault-Breguet Atlantic ASW and patrol aircraft, a bigger crew (in this case twelve crew members) is needed to process all the information gained from the aircraft's search equipment and man the aircraft on its long patrol flights. These shore-based patrol aircraft usually feature a fuselage weapons bay which carries ASW weapons.

Right: The latest version of the basic Dassault-Breguet Atlantic shore-based ASW patrol aircraft, configured for missile carrying
Below: The Lockheed S-3A Viking carrier-borne anti-submarine warfare patrol and attack aircraft

12
The Attack Aircraft Cockpit

The cockpit of the modern attack aircraft is different to that of the attack aircraft of the past in several important ways, not least in the amount of sophisticated avionics built into it. Indeed, some attack aircraft feature so much equipment to help them perform their particular tasks that a second crew member is required, such as in the General Dynamics F-111 and the Grumman A-6 Intruder, to work all the systems and gain the greatest benefit from them. In such cases the second crew member performs tasks dealing with such functions as

navigation and weapon aiming and delivery, while the pilot flies the aircraft and works the various systems which help him to do this. In the case of the F-111 and A-6, these include very sophisticated equipment due to the extremely demanding long-range day/night adverse weather low-altitude attack capabilities of these aircraft.

In comparison, the A-10A has rather simpler avionics, which can be easily worked by just the pilot himself without the need for a second crew member, and which are well tailored to the Thunderbolt II's close support attack missions. As well as the standard flight instruments, among which are the airspeed indicator, altimeter, and aircraft attitude indicator, there are the engine gauges, radio controls, and special features which include the television display for guidance of the aircraft's Maverick missiles and the Head-Up Display (HUD). The latter is a vitally important piece of equipment, for it projects all the relevant flight information and weapon-aiming details into the pilot's direct line of sight — thus preventing him from having to look down into the cockpit at his normal flight instruments, a factor of great importance as he can therefore keep his head up, visually flying the aircraft while looking for potential targets and ensuring that he can keep a watch for enemy aircraft that might be in the area.

Different attack aircraft might carry a different version of the basic HUD, designed to show the type of data applicable to their particular attack missions, but all HUDs have the same primary function of giving the pilot as much information in his direct line of sight as he needs for the particular phase of flight in which he is engaged.

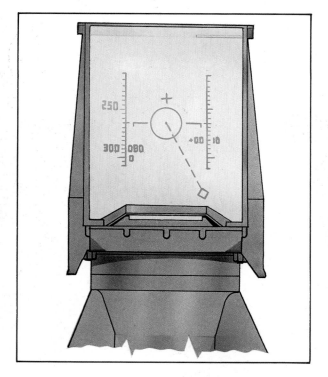

Right: The cockpit interior of the Fairchild A-10A Thunberbolt II, the aircraft featured on pages 22-23

Left: The type of information presented to the A-10A pilot by the HUD

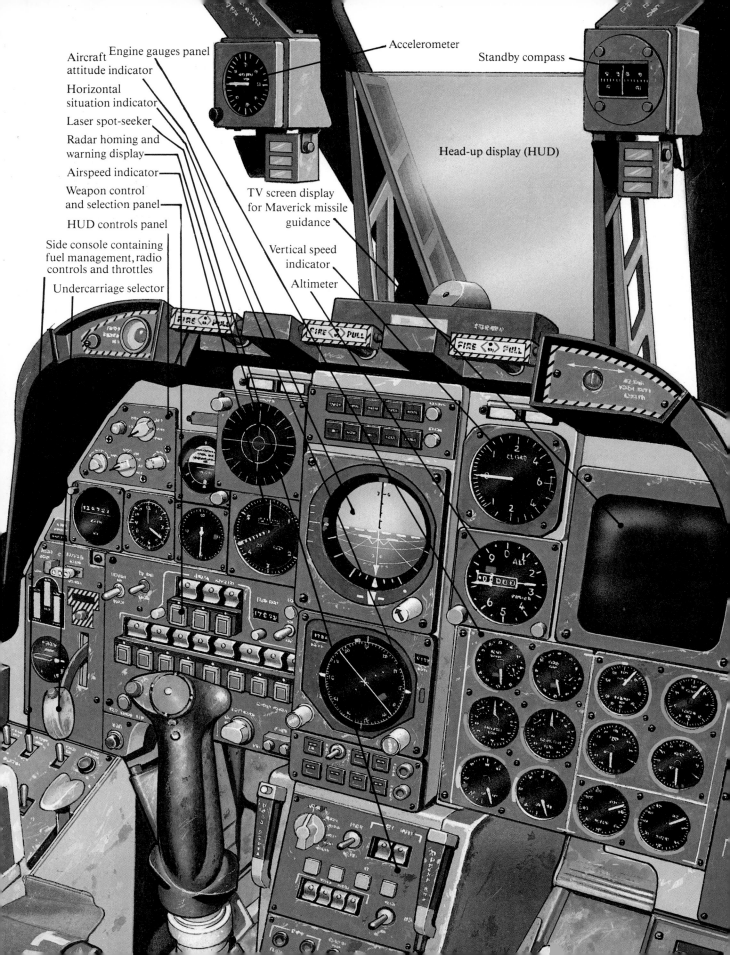

Aircraft
attitude indicator

Engine gauges panel

Accelerometer

Standby compass

Horizontal
situation indicator

Laser spot-seeker

Radar homing and
warning display

Airspeed indicator

Weapon control
and selection panel

HUD controls panel

Side console containing
fuel management, radio
controls and throttles

Undercarriage selector

Head-up display (HUD)

TV screen display
for Maverick missile
guidance

Vertical speed
indicator

Altimeter

13 Attack Aircraft Weapons (1)

Laser-guided versions rely on the target being illuminated by a laser designator on the ground or from the air so that the missile's laser seeker can home in on the target. A variation of this is the French Aérospatiale AS 30L missile, which is carried by the French Jaguar. It has laser guidance, the launch aircraft itself carrying a laser designator pod to illuminate the target for the missile, plus a television camera which the pilot uses to locate the target. It has infrared capability, which means it can be used even at night.

There are many different types of weapons available for use by modern attack aircraft, depending on the type of mission that the aircraft is tasked with and the type of targets that it is attacking. The weapons range from relatively simple and straightforward unguided bombs which can also be used by bombers, to more sophisticated guided missiles and special munitions. Some aircraft can also carry nuclear bombs similar to those on pages 14-15.

Guided air-to-ground missiles

The missiles carried by attack aircraft are generally much smaller than those carried by bombers and are designed to attack tactical targets in and around the battlefield or behind the enemy lines. Guided air-to-ground missiles (AGMs) give a vital "stand-off" capability to their launch aircraft, keeping the aircraft away from the target's defenses, but with the ability to be guided over some distance to the target by such means as television or laser systems. The Hughes AGM-65 Maverick has several different versions, some using television guidance — as those used by the A-10A — with a range of up to 7.8 miles (13 km), others use laser or IR guidance.

The television guidance relies on the aircraft's pilot visually identifying the target, flying towards it and moving the missile's television seeker until the target appears in the center of the cockpit television monitor. The target can then be locked onto and the missile fired; its seeker subsequently provides guidance to its moving tail surfaces to keep it on target.

The Maverick missile

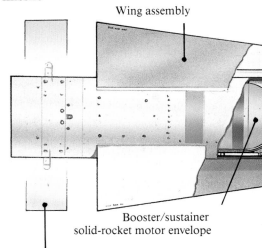

Wing assembly

Booster/sustainer solid-rocket motor envelope

Flight control surface on hydraulic actuation system

A Mirage carrying one of the French AS 30 family of missiles

Guided bombs

As well as the ordinary unguided bomb, there are several guided adaptations of these standard bombs, most of which use laser guidance in the form of add-on laser seekers at the bomb's nose and fins at the rear to aid the weapon's "flight" to the target. There are also infrared and television-guided bombs used in action in a similar fashion to guided missiles using such guidance means; for instance, the HOBOS or Homing Bomb System conversion. A further adaptation, the guided glide bomb, is a conversion from an ordinary unguided bomb but with cruciform wings allowing it to "fly" over greater distances to its target — as far as 4.8 miles (8 km), even when launched at low level.

GBU-15 glide bomb

Thermal battery

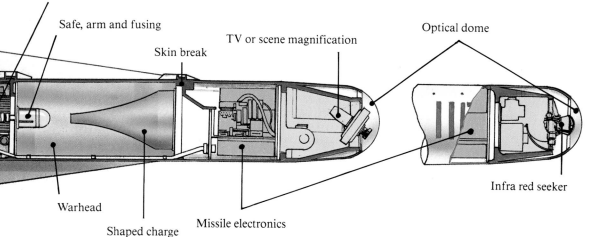

Safe, arm and fusing

Skin break

TV or scene magnification

Optical dome

Warhead

Shaped charge

Missile electronics

Infra red seeker

The HOBOS bomb conversion

Control power units

Hinged control surfaces

Thermal batteries

Auto pilot

Main fuse

Suspension lugs

Original MK 84 bomb

Guidance section

Seeker optics

E O window

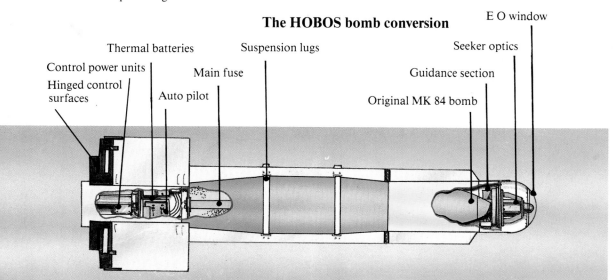

14 Attack Aircraft Weapons (2)

Anti-ship and anti-submarine warfare weapons

The anti-ship weapons carried by attack aircraft are much smaller than those carried by Soviet bombers. In addition to anti-ship attack missiles, anti-submarine warfare (ASW) weapons such as homing torpedoes, depth bombs and mines can be carried by a wide range of patrol and ASW aircraft.

Anti-ship missiles such as the Aérospatiale AM 39 Exocet are extremely effective against such difficult targets as modern warships, as was demonstrated during the Falkland Islands conflict in 1982 when Argentine-operated missiles proved very successful against ships of the British Task Force when launched from Super Etendard maritime attack aircraft. On a typical mission, the missile is capable of receiving full details of its target — such as the target's range and bearing — from the attack aircraft, which has previously located the target using its own nose-mounted radar. After launch, the missile assumes a cruise phase in which inertial navigation guides it towards the target at low level. When some 6 miles (10 km) from the target, the missile's active radar seeker locks onto the target, the terminal phase of flight at the target being achieved at sea-skimming height in which the missile's radar altimeter keeps a watch on its altitude and thus prevents it flying into the sea. Like the missiles on the previous pages, Exocet is rocket-powered, and can fly up to 42 miles (70 km). Instead of missiles, ASW work against submerged submarines is carried out with weapons such as depth bombs and homing torpedoes. Typical examples of both types are illustrated, these being used by such US Navy aircraft as the S-3A Viking.

Special weapons and munitions

Special types of weapon including the Cluster Bomb Unit (CBU), and rocket pods with associated ground attack rockets are available for use by attack aircraft. The CBU looks like an ordinary unguided bomb, but it contains within its

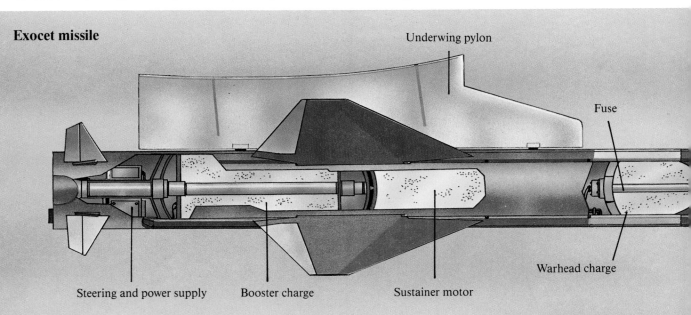

Exocet missile

Underwing pylon

Fuse

Warhead charge

Sustainer motor

Booster charge

Steering and power supply

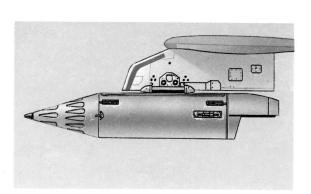

Rocket Pod

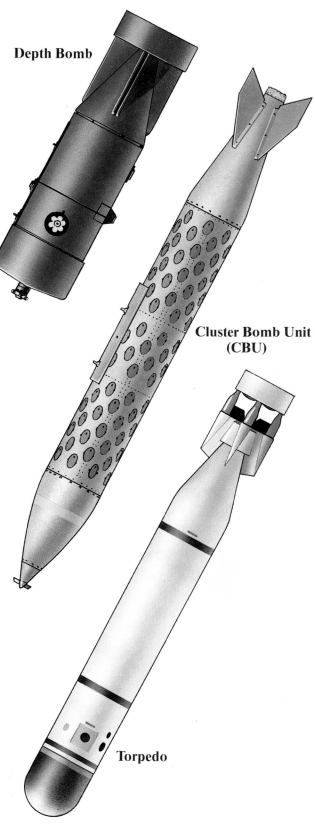

Depth Bomb

**Cluster Bomb Unit
(CBU)**

Torpedo

casing many small munitions which are ejected after release from the aircraft to cause damage over a wide area to targets such as tanks and soft-skinned vehicles. They either explode on impact or have a time fuse or other triggering mechanism which might set them off some time after being dropped. The rocket pod contains a number of small compact missiles which are unguided but provide a useful amount of firepower when released at such targets as vehicles or fixed lightly-protected installations. Each rocket has fin stabilizers, which are folded when stored in the pod but open out after launch to give stability during flight.

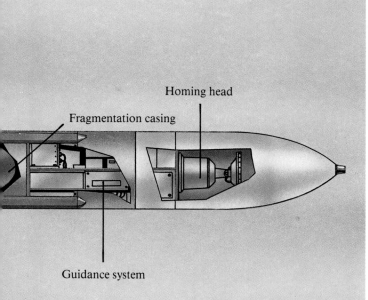

Homing head

Fragmentation casing

Guidance system

15 Battlefield Support Missions

Missile Attack

Gunnery Attack

In order to support ground forces on the battlefield, attack aircraft assigned to close-support missions have to be very rugged to avoid being shot down by the heavy enemy anti-aircraft fire that they will have to fly through while performing their missions. They must be able to co-ordinate with friendly land forces to ensure they are used in the right place at the right time; for example, against an enemy motorized advance which threatens to break through the friendly forces' lines.

In a typical attack, two A-10As would work together, flying to the battlefield at low level from bases close to the front-line, using the terrain as a natural cover to avoid being spotted and shot at by the enemy, until breaking cover to attack their targets.

In a Joint Air Attack Team (JAAT) operation, the A-10As would co-ordinate with US Army Bell AH-1S Cobra helicopter gunships; the helicopters would attack the enemy's anti-aircraft defenses, drawing their fire, while the A-10As would concentrate on attacking the enemy's tanks. The tanks might be marked out for them by laser-equipped ground forces, a FAC aircraft or a scout helicopter, which illuminates the target for the A-10A by laser designator and also draws fire from the attacking aircraft. The A-10A picks up the radiated laser energy from the designated target with its laser seeker and attacks it with its GAU-8/A cannon or Maverick ASMs using the Maverick's own guidance means; an X marker on the A-10A's HUD displays the target's position.

Such a method is used by many attack aircraft

Above: The A-10A on its low level gunnery and missile attack approaches the target from its normal height of below 99 feet (30 m), then temporarily breaks cover and pops up to around 500 feet (150 m) to make an attack on a tank, using its GAU-8/A cannon, or at longer ranges, its Maverick missiles.

Right: The way in which the A-10A can be used in direct support of land elements, working together with other friendly airborne forces

operating in the close support role where FAC facilities exist or indeed if the aircraft carries the equipment to designate the target itself.

16 Gunship and Longer-Range Attack Missions

Gunship missions

The attack missions performed by special gunship modifications were perfected during the Vietnam War. Missions were frequently flown at night rather than during the daytime, and to concentrate the fire of the aircraft's weapons, the pilot would fly in a large counterclockwise circle around the target. This ensured that all the aircraft's specially-fitted machine-guns and cannons, which fire from the left-hand side of the aircraft's fuselage, could be brought to bear continually by the pilot. This method is very effective against targets such as lightly-armored vehicles and infantry positions, but a potential drawback is that the gunship is vulnerable to ground fire, especially if the enemy employs surface-to-air missiles.

Longer-range attack missions of the Jaguar and the F-111

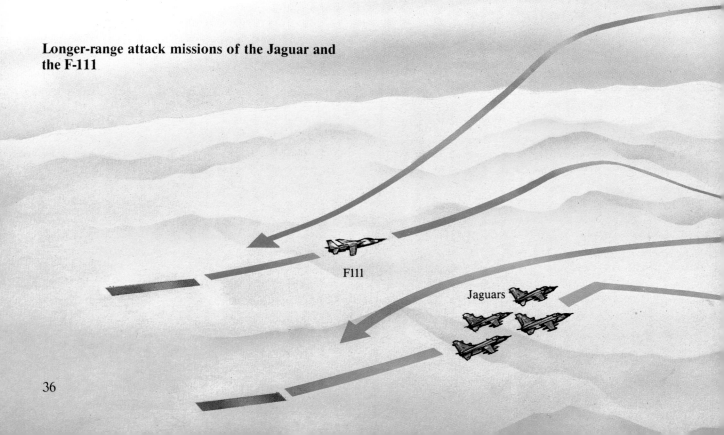

F111

Jaguars

Longer-range attack missions

Attack missions flown by specialized aircraft, such as the Jaguar and the all-weather day/night A-6 Intruder, take a completely different form. In the case of the Jaguar, low-level missions are flown using the aircraft's sophisticated inertial navigation and attack equipment. Attacks are usually preplanned, the location of the target having been established before the mission begins, and the route flown to it predetermined. This relies on good reconnaissance. All relevant details of locations and planned course are fed into the aircraft's onboard computers. A mission is usually flown at low level and in stages to deceive and confuse the enemy's defenses as to the location of the target being attacked; at each turning point, the pilot automatically receives details from his navigation equipment of the point at which to turn by an X marker on his HUD. Once in the target area, the run in to the target is made from a prominent landmark called the Initial Point (IP). On the pilot's HUD, weapons aiming instructions are given, together with the exact point at which the weapons should be released for best results, the aircraft's computers working this out automatically.

On such missions, more than one aircraft would normally fly on the same attack (unless nuclear bombs were being carried, when the aircraft would fly alone). Very different to these are the low-level attacks flown by all-weather attack aircraft like the A-6 Intruder and F-111. The F-111, in particular, almost always operate singly, as during the Vietnam War, and unlike most other attack aircraft require no backup in the form of electronic support aircraft, tankers, fighter cover, or FAC guidance.

The success of the F-111s mission is based on the aircraft's TFR keeping it as close to the ground as possible to avoid detection by the enemy's radar defenses, and its sophisticated inertial navigation equipment which guides it to the target. Missions may be carried out at night because the pilot does not necessarily need to see where he is going as the aircraft is piloted automatically by the TFR whose instructions provide the necessary control responses. Weapon release can again be computerized, the second crew member providing any necessary visual sighting functions.

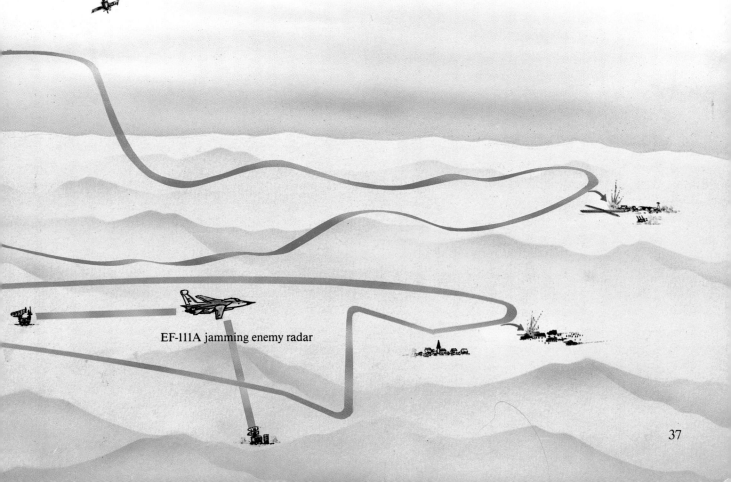

EF-111A jamming enemy radar

17 Maritime Attack Missions

Maritime attack

Missions against surface ships can be carried out by bombers if they are configured for this type of role, but the only country to use bombers in any numbers for this task is the Soviet Union. In the West, airborne anti-shipping missions are assigned mainly to attack aircraft that carry the generally smaller-type anti-ship missiles like the Exocet (see pages 32-33). Anti-ship missions using these missiles are usually carried out by high-speed attack aircraft, either carrier- or shore-based, like the French Dassault-Breguet Super Etendard, Hawker Siddeley Buccaneer, and a maritime-attack version of the Jaguar.

Some patrol aircraft, such as later versions of the French Dessault-Breguet Atlantic (see page 27), can also carry anti-ship missiles, which they can use against the hostile ships that they have located during their patrol. These patrol aircraft, however, usually carry weapons suited to ASW, as do specialist attack aircraft like the S-3A Viking.

The locating of enemy submarines is a very difficult task if they are submerged, but there are several methods the searching aircraft can use to find the submarine. The MAD boom, with its in-built sensors, searches for any magnetic deviation in the earth's magnetic field caused by the large metal mass of a submarine. Sonobuoys can be dropped to listen out for the sound of a passing submarine ("passive" search), or send out acoustic waves that reflect back off a submarine ("active" search). In both cases, the buoys have a communications link with the aircraft that dropped them

to give details of any contacts made. The aircraft's own large nose radar and other sensors such as infrared equipment can search for a submarine's periscope on the surface, or indeed can be used to locate surface ships. The aircraft's onboard computers can show, once a potential submarine target has been located, where it is located so that the aircraft's weapons can be launched to best advantage. Among these, anti-submarine depth bombs are dropped so that their explosions under water create shock waves that can damage the submarine's hull.

In the case of anti-ship missiles, the launch aircraft detects the target with its nose radar, gives the missile's systems all relevant details, and then launches the missile; the weapon's own radar provides terminal guidance when close to the target while flying very close to the water. The launch aircraft can therefore stand off from the target, not needing to fly near its defenses, and can escape from the general area as soon as possible.

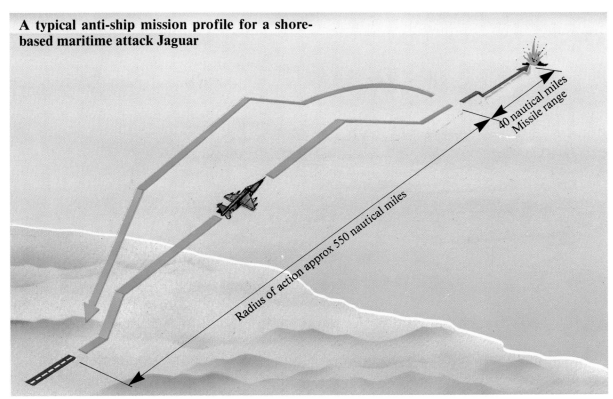

A typical anti-ship mission profile for a shore-based maritime attack Jaguar

Radius of action approx 550 nautical miles

40 nautical miles
Missile range

A submerged submarine being detected by a S-3A patrol aircraft using its MAD equipment, both types of sonobuoys, and radar. It is launching a torpedo and a depth bomb.

18 Additional Roles and Derivatives

When front-line bombers and attack aircraft reach the end of their operational lives and are replaced by more modern types, they are often converted for special duties. Similarly, some aircraft still in service form the basis of special modifications or conversions, which create a wholly new version of the basic type able to perform different functions from the standard bomber or attack aircraft from which they are derived.

Target-towing

A useful role that some former bombers have been put to is that of target-towing. This is an important role not only for air-to-air gunnery and simulated missile firing practice but also for surface firing training from the ground or from warships. One bomber converted into this role is the BAC Canberra. It can tow a number of specially-designed targets from underwing pods that can reel out the targets some distance behind to ensure that the Canberra itself is not hit when the targets are fired at.

Special test-beds

Several bombers have been put to use as engine testbeds. The purpose of these conversions is to test new engines that are being developed before they are fitted into modern warplanes. The converted bombers carry special equipment to test the performance of the new engines. With the bomber's large and multi-engined layout, it is possible for them to carry an extra engine without danger.

Airborne refueling

Due to their large size and internal capacity, bombers have been ideal for conversion into in-flight refueling tanker aircraft. Extra fuel cells are added inside the bomber, often within the fuselage instead of bombs, and in-flight refueling is carried out by trailing a long fuel pipe down to the aircraft receiving fuel, which itself carries a nozzle which connects to the tanker's fuel pipe.

Major conversions

Special conversions of several current attack aircraft have led to completely new versions dedicated to ECM work. These aircraft carry large amounts of special receiving equipment that detects enemy transmissions, radar, and related electronic emissions, and jams them with its on-board electronic equipment and transmitters. In this way, they can provide protection for attack aircraft that would otherwise be detected if they did not have their own extensive ECM equipment.

A Canberra towing a target

Bottom: A Boeing B-47 bomber, now long out of front-line service, testing the Canadian Orenda Iroquois PS-13 turbojet engine in a pod mounted on the rear fuselage

Below: A Soviet Tupolev Tu-16 tanker trails its fuel pipe from one wingtip and hooks up to the wingtip nozzle of a standard Tupolev Tu-16 bomber.

Above: The Grumman EA-6B Prowler derivative for ECM work of the A-6 Intruder attack aircraft, with aerodynamic changes for its electronic systems and two extra crew members to work this equipment

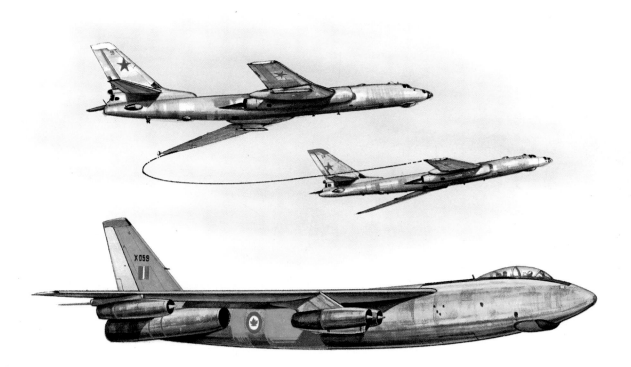

41

19
Bomber and Attack Aircraft Cost and Distribution

Many countries operate attack aircraft, some in large numbers as can be seen on the map. Bombers, however, are only operated by a small number of countries, including the superpowers, some of the larger countries, and friends of the superpowers. This is due both to the cost of these aircraft and the related equipment that is required to properly operate them and because few countries are likely to need their truly long-range strategic capacity. Attack aircraft are far more useful to most countries because of their tactical roles on and around the battlefield and behind the enemy lines; they are also much less expensive.

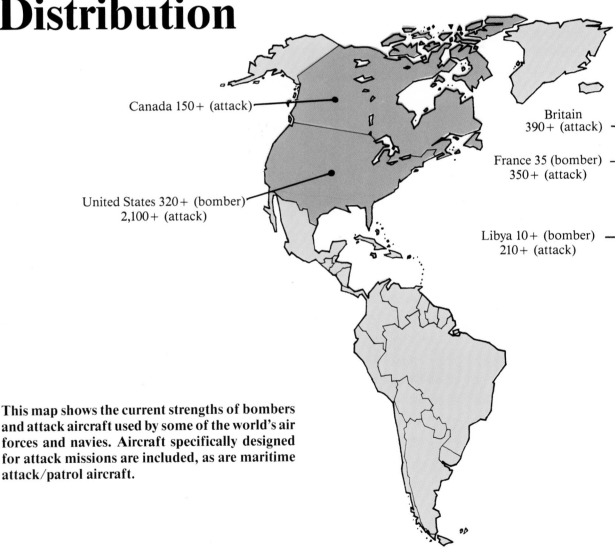

Canada 150+ (attack)

Britain 390+ (attack)

France 35 (bomber) 350+ (attack)

United States 320+ (bomber) 2,100+ (attack)

Libya 10+ (bomber) 210+ (attack)

This map shows the current strengths of bombers and attack aircraft used by some of the world's air forces and navies. Aircraft specifically designed for attack missions are included, as are maritime attack/patrol aircraft.

When the SEPECAT Jaguar was being built in quantity during the early 1970's, a single aircraft cost below $2 million. Since then costs have increased for all combat aircraft, and the cost of an aircraft like the Grumman A-6E Intruder is over $36 million. However, this price compares well with the latest price for an EA-6B Prowler of over $66 million.

In contrast, the cost of a new bomber is massive. The price quoted for the first production B-1B bombers was $419.5 million each. This compares with the 1943-44 price for a Consolidated B-24J Liberator heavy bomber, a successful US design used during the Second World War, which was $210,943. The weapons used by bombers and attack aircraft are also expensive — early versions of the AGM-65 Maverick were some $60,000 each — together with their bases, whether on shore or aircraft carriers, which generally need to be fitted out with vast quantities of support and maintenance equipment. Extra forward bases may have to be built, as well, for attack aircraft, these being close to a potential battle zone to ensure that the aircraft are able to get to the scene of battle quickly.

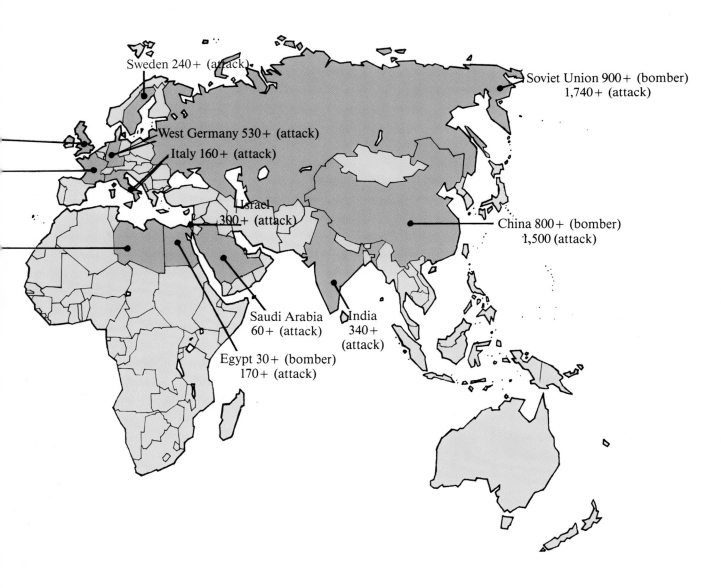

Sweden 240+ (attack)

Soviet Union 900+ (bomber)
1,740+ (attack)

West Germany 530+ (attack)

Italy 160+ (attack)

Israel 300+ (attack)

China 800+ (bomber)
1,500 (attack)

Saudi Arabia 60+ (attack)

India 340+ (attack)

Egypt 30+ (bomber)
170+ (attack)

20 Looking to the Future

New developments and technological advances are taking place all the time in the fields of bomber and attack aircraft design and technology as well as in weapons research and electronics. These advances will greatly alter the design of warplanes in the future and lead to new generations of aircraft and weapons.

Future bomber designs

One of the most important developments in bomber design is in the field of "stealth" technology. This aims at producing designs which are so carefully streamlined that radar has difficulty in detecting them because they have fewer of the sharp edges and large flat surfaces that on normal designs are liable to be "seen" by radar. Two possible future bomber designs under study are illustrated. One design (top) features a fully retracting wing which pivots at its center; in normal flight and for takeoff and landing, the wing is mounted as on a normal aircraft. But for low-level supersonic flight to the target, the wing is pivoted to lie flat (retracted) along the top of the fuselage, all the required lift coming from the fuselage in this folded configuration. Such an aircraft is also much more difficult to see coming from the ground due to its folded appearance.

The aircraft's general layout is rather more conventional in the second design (below) but still retains a very blended streamlined shape which, like other future "stealth" types, would feature radar-absorbant covering to further reduce radar's effectiveness to locate it and special non-reflective paint. Another important feature is the position of the engine air intake above the fuselage, where it is shielded by the airframe and thus ground radar cannot easily detect its otherwise obvious contours.

Future weapons

Large advances are similarly being made with the weapons used by bombers and attack aircraft. Important among these are the projects aimed at providing a more efficient means of propulsion for rockets and missiles. This involves replacing the standard rocket motor with powerplants such as an air-breathing ram rocket, which mixes air taken in through side air intakes with fuel-enriched gases produced by a solid rocket fuel to produce powerful efficient high-energy jet propulsion.

The Advanced Strategic Air-Launched Missile is based on similar principles but features a specially-designed layout with no wings, in which the missile's body shape generates its own lift.

Of future importance for attack aircraft is the revolutionary hypervelocity missile (HVM). This is a very high speed (Mach 4.5) missile-shaped rod, which will hit its target, using laser guidance from the launch aircraft, so fast and with so much force that no warhead is needed.

Left: Air-breathing ram rocket powered missile

Right: The proposed layout of a missile projected for use by the A-10A Thunderbolt II

Below right: Hypervelocity missile (HVM)

44

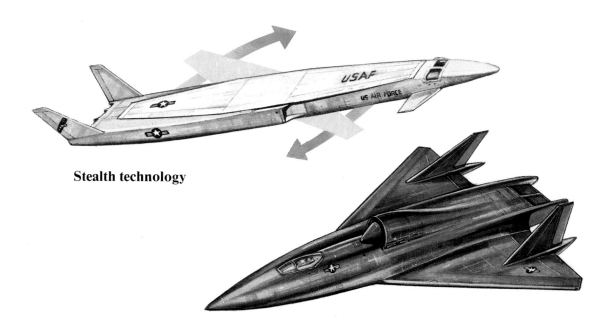

Stealth technology

**Advanced Strategic Air-Launched Missile
(ASALM)**

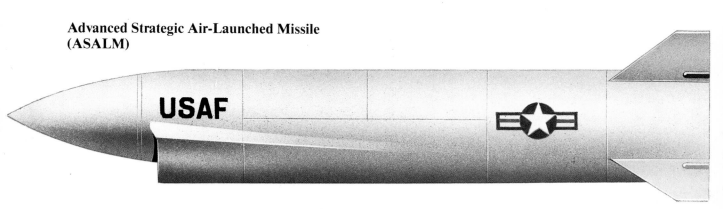

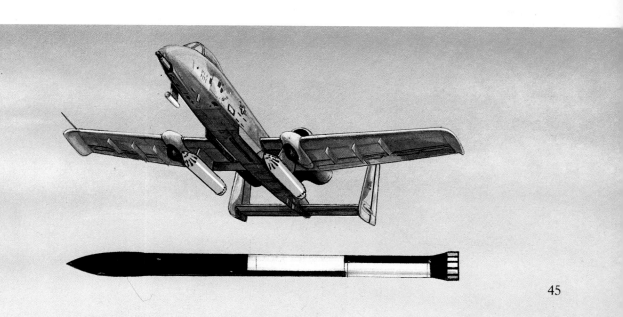

Glossary

ACTIVE RADAR
Aircraft, missile, or ground radars that emit high frequency radio pulses which are reflected back from the object or objects that they are searching for

ACTIVE SONAR
An 'active' search for submarines consists of the sonobuoy emitting acoustic waves, which reflect back from the submarine and are detected by the sonobuoy to give details of the submarine's position and other relevant information

AFTERBURNER
In order to dramatically increase the power given out by jet engines for short periods such as take-off or for fast speed bursts, fuel is injected directly into the hot jet stream as it leaves the engine's turbine (see 'Turbojet/Turbofan'), thus producing additional thrust. After-burning consumes a great deal of fuel and is used for short periods only.

AGM
Air-to-Ground Missile. 'AGM' is also used in the US system of designation to indicate the type and role of weapons, in this case air-to-ground missiles of such diverse types as the Hughes AGM-65 Maverick series and the Boeing AGM-86B ALCM.

ALCM
Air-Launched Cruise Missile, the name given to the Boeing AGM-86B nuclear-armed cruise missile, carried by the US Air Force's B-52G, B-52H, and B-1B bombers. The term 'air-launched cruise missile' can also be applied to other weapons of this specific type, a new Soviet contemporary of the AGM-86B being the AS-15.

ASALM —
Advanced Strategic Air-Launched Missile, the projected strategic missile for future use by US bombers which uses recent technology in aerodynamics and propulsion

ASW
Anti-Submarine Warfare, a term covering all aspects of the detection and attacking of enemy submarines by ships and aircraft. The aircraft involved in ASW work are as diverse as the Lockheed S-3A Viking carrier-borne ASW patrol and attack aircraft and the shore-based Dassault-Breguet Atlantic ASW and patrol aircraft.

AVIONICS
From *avi*ation elect*ronics*, the science concerned with the development of electronics and electrical devices for use in aircraft. The term is sometimes used generally to embrace the aircraft's electronic and cockpit equipment and displays.

B—
Bomber, in the US system of designation to indicate the type and role of a particular warplane. This includes the Boeing B-52 Stratofortress and Rockwell B-1B bombers; the latter has a lower designation number than the B-52, which preceded it, due to being included in the new numbering system instituted in 1962, the B-52 coming from the numbering system current before that time. The "B" naming process is also used in the West to describe Soviet warplanes; all code-names for Soviet bombers beginning with the letter "B", such as the Tupolev Tu-95 "Bear" and the Tu-26 "Backfire" bombers.

BAC
British Aircraft Corporation, the company formed from the amalgamation of several British aviation companies in the 1960's, which itself became a part of British Aerospace during the 1970's

BAe
British Aerospace, the British nationalized aircraft company created from several formerly independent companies during the 1970's

CHAFF
Radar reflective material, usually made up of many strips of aluminized fiberglass or foil, cut to fractions of the wavelength of the enemy radars to be jammed. Radars are unable to distinguish between this type of material dropped in clouds by aircraft and the aircraft themselves, thus confusing the radar and obscuring the aircraft that it is attempting to detect and track.

CONVENTIONAL
Applied to weapons, a term meaning non-nuclear, having a high-explosive and not a nuclear warhead

ECM
Electronic Counter Measures, the science of investigating and identifying and then jamming, confusing, or otherwise disturbing an enemy's radars and related electronic equipment by mainly electronic means

FLIR
Forward-Looking Infra-Red, a sensor often carried with LLTV equipment on some attack aircraft and bombers. It can be used in conditions up to near or total darkness and provides for the aircraft's crew on a cockpit monitor a picture of the ground ahead of the aircraft while flying at low level. The picture is composed of a scene made up of images ranging from black to white, cool objects being nearer to black while hotter objects — such as a moving vehicle — are lighter shades or even white. FLIR equipment is thus an aid to detecting potential targets even at night in addition to allowing the aircraft to fly safely much closer to the ground than would otherwise be possible.

HOBOS
Homing Bomb System, the name given to the US program in which standard unguided conventional bombs are converted by means of add-on components to give them a guided capability. The conversion usually consists of a nose seeker of the TV or IR guidance type plus movable control fins fitted at the rear of the bomb to help it 'maneuver' onto the target. A developed version of this principle is the guided glide bomb, which features additional add-on cruciform wings which give the ordinary bomb to which they are affixed the ability to be launched some distance from the target and then 'fly' to it, being able to do this even though it does not carry any form of power plant or engine.

HUD
Head-Up Display, the cockpit instrument which projects all relevant flight and weapon-aiming details into the pilot's line of sight to prevent him from having to repeatedly look down at his normal flight instruments

INERTIAL NAVIGATION
A self-contained system within the aircraft or missile needing no outside communication during flight with ground stations, launch aircraft, etc. It contains three major components — a platform, containing accelerometers, a gyroscopic frame, and a computer. The accelerometers measure the aircraft or missile's acceleration, each acceleration signal being converted into distance covered by firstly determining the aircraft or missile's total change in velocity which, added to the known initial velocity, gives the craft's velocity at any given time, and secondly determining the craft's total change in position which, added to the known initial position of the flight in latitude and longitude, gives the craft's present position at any given time. Such information as direction and distance covered can thus be determined. The gyroscopic frame contains three gyroscopes which constantly work to stabilize the accelerometers' platform to ensure that true and accurate readings are always given. The computer carries out all the necessary calculations from the readings taken by the system. When linked to the flight controls of an aircraft or missile, the system can give corrective information which ensures that the craft stays on its planned course if the system senses that it has strayed off course. Such a guidance is potentially very accurate, not only for weapon delivery but for navigation in general.

INS
Inertial Navigation System (see above)

IR
Infra-Red

JAMMING
The effect of disrupting or confusing an enemy's radars, communications, and allied equipment, achieved mainly by electronic means but also by the use of such materials as chaff

Kt
Kiloton, a nuclear warhead's explosive power, equal to the power of 1,000 tons of TNT

LLTV

Low-Light TeleVision, also sometimes Low-Light Level TeleVision, a device carried by some attack aircraft and bombers consisting of a television camera which is linked to a cockpit television monitor. This is used to give a picture of the ground being flown over enroute to the target at low level, in low light conditions or even in the kind of darkness prevalent on a starlit night. The equipment can also be used to identify potential targets and is often used in conjunction with a FLIR sensor.

MAD

Magnetic Anomoly Detection, comprising Magnetic Anomoly Detector equipment as carried by attack and patrol aircraft involved in ASW work. The MAD equipment is usually carried at the end of a boom at the tail end of the aircraft to keep it away from the magnetic disturbance caused by the aircraft itself. Carried over the sea in this way, the equipment is able to detect any local variation in the Earth's own magnetic field caused by a submerged submarine, whose large metal mass creates such variations.

PASSIVE RADAR

Passive, or more normally semi-active radars, do not themselves emit radio pulses in the way that active radars do but home in on radar signals reflected from the target — these radar signals having been directed at the target by an active radar which the semi-active radar can then detect. Such semi-active radars are often carried by missiles, which home in on the active radar signals aimed at and reflected from the target by the missile's launch aircraft.

PASSIVE SONAR

A 'passive' search for submarines is where the sonobuoy contains very sensitive listening devices which simply listen for the sound of the submarine; they therefore do not emit accoustic waves in the way that sonobuoys do on an 'active' search for submarines.

PORT

Left-hand

PR

PhotoReconnaissance, as used in the designation of British aircraft engaged in this particular role and including the BAC Canberra PR Mk 9 photoreconnaissance version of the standard Canberra bomber

RADAR

(From *radio detection and ranging*), the electronic system that can detect an aircraft — or, in some radar types, features on the ground — hidden by darkness, distance, or cloud cover, by the transmission of extremely high-frequency radio pulses. These reflect back to the transmitting radar from the object that it is attempting to detect, thus showing the position, distance and other features of the object. For bomber and attack aircraft it can be used to show objects and even targets on the ground, and a particularly useful application is the TFR (terrain-following radar) which 'pictures' the ground ahead of the aircraft flying at low-level and at night, detecting the features of the ground ahead and thus allowing the aircraft to fly very close to the ground without hitting it, showing the objects in its path so that aircraft can fly over or around them. These are active, emitting radars (see also 'Active'; for non-emitting radars see 'Passive').

SAM

Surface-to-Air Missile

SRAM

Short-Range Attack Missile, the name given to the Boeing AGM-69A nuclear-armed missile, carried by versions of the Boeing B-52 Stratofortress and the Rockwell B-1B

STAND-OFF

The term used in connection with guided missiles and also guided bombs with a significant range, which can be released by the launch aircraft, either an attack aircraft or bomber, some distance from the target but can still hit the target through guidance means even at this distance. The attacking aircraft can thus 'stand-off' from the target (ie it does not have to *closely* approach the target), thus avoiding the target's defenses.

STARBOARD

Right-hand

STEALTH

One of the new technological advances in aircraft design aims to produce aircraft so carefully streamlined and blended that enemy radars find it difficult to detect them. They feature few of the sharp edges or prominent flat surfaces that on conventional aircraft are easily detected by radar. Such streamlined shapes are also difficult to detect visually, and they sometimes feature engines mounted above the airframe to prevent the powerplants' hot IR signature from being detected from the ground and hide their prominent contours from ground radar.

STRATEGIC TARGETS

Objectives which lie deep behind the battlefield in the enemy country's heartland and consist of cities, major industrial complexes, ports, and other large permanent fixed targets. They are the targets of bombers, which have the range and the ability to carry the large long-range weapons used to strike at these targets, such weapons often being nuclear-armed.

SUPERPOWERS

A term usually applied to the US and the Soviet Union

TACTICAL TARGETS

Military targets such as enemy forces and installations in and around the battlefield, and also behind the front lines but excluding the large, remote strategic targets which are the objectives of bombers. Attack aircraft fly on tactical missions.

TFR

Terrain-Following Radar (see 'Radar')

TNT

TriNitroToluene: a high explosive, often used as an equivalent measure of the explosive power of nuclear warheads

TU (TUPOLEV)

A Soviet designer and manufacturer of mainly bomber aircraft

TURBOJET/TURBOFAN

The turbojet is a jet engine in which a turbine-driven compressor draws in air at the engine air intake at the front of the engine and forces the compressed air into a combustion chamber, fuel being injected into this chamber and then ignited, the hot gases so produced subsequently rushing through and driving the turbine and then being ejected at the outlet nozzle at the rear. Forward thrust is created as a reaction to the rearward momentum of the exhaust gases. This type of engine has a high fuel consumption. A more recent development is the turbofan, in which some of the in-coming air is by-passed round the combustion chamber and accelerated rearwards by a turbine-operated fan to mix with the exhaust gases from the combustion chamber. This increases the air-mass flowing rearwards over that achieved in the turbojet, increasing thrust without increasing fuel consumption.

TURBOPROP

A hybrid engine type, producing jet thrust but also driving a propeller. The turboprop is used in some commercial aircraft, and some large military aircraft such as the Tupolev Tu-95 "Bear," this type of engine being efficient at the high altitudes that such an aircraft might operate and also gives a good power-to-weight ratio. The turboprop is basically similar to a turbojet engine, except that it has an added turbine behind the combustion chamber which absorbs much of the energy produced by the engine and drives the propeller by means of a shaft and speed-reducing gears.

Index